Everard Kempshall

Caldwell and the Revolution

A Historical Sketch of the First Presbyterian Church of Elizabeth....

Everard Kempshall

Caldwell and the Revolution
A Historical Sketch of the First Presbyterian Church of Elizabeth....

ISBN/EAN: 9783337116576

Printed in Europe, USA, Canada, Australia, Japan

Cover: Foto ©ninafisch / pixelio.de

More available books at **www.hansebooks.com**

The Centennial Anniversary of the Burning of
the Church Edifice of the First Presbyterian
Church of Elizabeth, New Jersey.

"Caldwell and the Revolution;"

A HISTORICAL SKETCH OF THE

FIRST PRESBYTERIAN CHURCH OF ELIZABETH,

PRIOR TO AND DURING THE WAR OF THE REVOLUTION;

BEING A DISCOURSE DELIVERED ON

SUNDAY, JANUARY 25th, 1880,

BY

REV. EVERARD KEMPSHALL, D. D.

PASTOR OF THE CHURCH.

Printed by Order of the Board of Trustees.

ELIZABETH, N. J.:
Elizabeth Daily Journal, Cor. Broad and Jersey Streets.
1880.

PREFATORY NOTE.

The following is an extract from the minutes of a meeting of the Session of the First Presbyterian Church of Elizabeth, N. J., held January 5th, 1880:

"On the last Sabbath of this month, being the 25th inst., occurs the one hundredth anniversary of the burning of the church-edifice of this congregation. It was set on fire by British soldiers, or by Tory refugees, on the night of January 25, 1780, and was totally consumed.

In the judgment of Session it is eminently fitting that some proper commemoration of so interesting an event, in the history of the town and of the church, should be made ; therefore, it is hereby

Resolved, That the Pastor be respectfully requested to preach a discourse on the evening of the 25th inst., upon the history of the First Church, up to and during the War of the American Revolution, and to arrange for such other services on that day as may appear in his judgment to be proper."

In pursuance of this action of the Session, a discourse was delivered on the morning of Sunday, January 25, by Reverend Professor Cameron, of Princeton College, on "Jonathan Dickinson and the College of New Jersey," and in the evening a discourse by the Pastor on "Caldwell and the Revolution."

The church was appropriately draped for the occasion with American flags and other insignia.

3

Professor Cameron's discourse was delivered in the presence of a large and interested congregation.

In the evening the church was thronged by citizens of Elizabeth and the vicinity, all available sitting and standing room being taken within a few moments after the doors were opened. The other Presbyterian congregations in the city were invited to participate in the evening service, and their churches were closed.

In the evening a choir of about thirty voices, under Mr. W. C. Williams, led the music. An opening piece, " Before Jehovah's Awful Throne," was sung. Professor Cameron invoked the Divine blessing, and the congregation then sang Hymn 124, " Praise Ye Jehovah's Name." Rev. E. C. Ray, of the Third Presbyterian Church, read the Song of Moses and the 127th Psalm, and Rev. Dr. W. C. Roberts, of Westminster Church, offered prayer. The choir then sang Mendelssohn's chorus, "Judge Me, O God." Then followed the sermon on " Caldwell and the Revolution" by Rev. E. Kempshall, D. D., Pastor of the church.

After the sermon, Rev. Hugh Smyth, of the Second Presbyterian Church, offered the closing prayer, and the choir and congregation sang " America," closing with the Doxology. Rev. Mr. Street, of Connecticut Farms, pronounced the benediction, and the exercises were closed.

The Session of the church subsequently passed a resolution requesting a copy of the discourse delivered by the Pastor on this memorable occasion for publication, and that the Trustees proceed to have the same published in pamphlet form.

In accordance with the request of the Session, the Trustees have caused this pamphlet to be printed.

"Caldwell and the Revolution."

"And the children of Judah prevailed, because they relied upon the Lord God of their fathers.—2 CHRON. XIII, 18.

On the night of the 25th of January, 1780, just one hundred years ago to-day, the church edifice which stood upon the spot where we are now assembled, was destroyed by fire. Tradition relates that the firing of the building was the act of a Tory refugee, whose parents were honored members of this church. It may be quite possible that, in the absence of positive evidence as to the person by whom this crime was committed, it was attributed to Cornelius Hetfield, Jr., because of the well-known intensity of his hatred for the patriots, and his readiness to engage as guide to any marauding party from Staten Island, which was during the Revolutionary War the stronghold of the British forces near New York, and the refuge of Tories and deserters. The *New Jersey Journal* (the first number of

The aim of the writer in this discourse has been simply to present a succinct statement of leading facts of interest in the history of this church, during the century which elapsed from its origin to the destruction of the church edifice in 1780 ; together with other incidents of local interest more immediately related to the War of the Revolution. For most of these facts the writer wishes to make acknowledgment, in the fullest manner, of his indebtedness to the Rev. E. F. Hatfield, D. D., in his most excellent work, "The History of Elizabeth." This general expression of obligation is made here, as it was not convenient to make it in every instance in the progress of the discourse.

5

which appeared Feb. 16th, 1779) of the 27th January, 1780, makes the following statement :

"A party of the enemy consisting of about three hundred infantry, under the command of Col. Van Buskirk, of the new levies, and about sixty dragoons, said to be under the command of Capt. Steward, with several refugees, the whole in number nearly 400, crossed on the ice from Staten Island to Trembly's Point, about three miles from Elizabeth Town, last Tuesday night. From thence they were conducted by Cornelius Hetfield, Job Hetfield and Smith Hetfield, their principal guides, the nearest and most retired route to Elizabeth Town. They entered the town in two divisions before the alarm was sounded. As soon as the troops that were in town (consisting of about sixty men), perceived their danger, they retreated; however, they took a Major (Major Williamson), who was commandant of the place, and two or three captains that lodged in town that night, and a few troops. They then set fire to the Presbyterian Meeting and Court House, which were consumed; plundered, insulted, and took off, some of the inhabitants, and retreated with great precipitation by the way of De Hart's Point, whose house they likewise consumed."

Washington speaks of the event two days after as " the late misfortune and disgrace at Elizabeth Town." The father of Cornelius Hetfield, Jr., had been a Trustee, and was then an Elder of the church. " As the son had destroyed their church edifice, so the father opened the doors of a large 'Red Store-house,' on the south side of the creek, near West Water Street, that belonged to him, which was fitted up for the purpose and used thenceforward as a meeting-house. This renegade son was a man of great energy of character, and of commanding influence among the refugees. During the previous two years he had resided on Staten Island, continually watching opportunities to molest and capture his former friends and neighbors." He was afterward tried for the murder of one Stephen Ball during the war, and barely escaped being hanged. In this connection we may add, that in an unsuccessful attempt to capture Gov. Livingston, then residing here (in the house now occupied by Col. John Kean), and Maxwell's brigade, made by the British on the morning of February 25th, 1779, the barracks and the Presbyterian parsonage, then used as barracks, were in the rage of the enemy at their disappointment, set on fire and burned down. This destruction of the parsonage involved the irreparable loss of all the church records, save a few account books which were lodged in some other place. The school-house, or Academy, adjoining the Presbyterian burying-ground, which had been used for storing provisions for the troops, was also fired and destroyed. These acts of wanton destruction of property which would be regarded as sacred under the ideas which obtain now in civilized warfare, may serve to illustrate the reckless, unscrupulous, malicious character, and we may add, the fruitlessness of the attacks which were made by the British upon Eastern New Jersey during the Revolutionary War. We may form a very fair idea of the external appearance of the church-building which was standing here in 1780, from a description given by Captain Wm. C. DeHart in his "Passages in the History of Elizabeth Town." "The Court House was a small, frame, shingle-covered building, which had never been adorned with paint, and in the same condition and style of architecture was the adjacent building, the Presbyterian Meeting-house, both of which respectively occu-

7

pied the ground whereon now stand the structures devoted to the same object. The church was ornamented by a steeple surmounted by a ball and weathercock, furnished also with a clock. It was the most conspicuous and the most valuable building in the town, hallowed as the structure in which their pilgrim fathers worshiped God, and in which they themselves, so many of them, had been consecrated to God in baptism, and in which the great and revered Dickinson, the honored Spencer, and the still more renowned Whitfield had preached God's word."

There is good reason for believing that the General Assemblies held under the Proprietors, sat in this house; and that so also did the Supreme Court. In 1767, the pulpit was ornamented by the ladies with an "elegant set of curtains, which cost twenty-seven pounds sterling." For many years there was a part of the church not seated, probably reserved as a lobby for the accommodation of those who attended the Legislature and the Courts. The precise date at which the first church-edifice was erected on this spot, cannot be ascertained. In the early settlement of the town, the "town-house" and the "meeting-house" were one. It is more than probable that one of the first public concerns of the original Associates was the building of their "meeting-house." As early as February 19th, 1665, they held a "meeting-court," at which the whole town was present, and sixty-five men took the oath of allegiance and fidelity to King Charles II. A house-of-worship had most likely been built before this date; nothing can now be determined as to its size, cost, or arrangement.

In a letter addressed to the *Elizabeth Daily Journal*

of May 12, 1873, Dr. Hatfield says: "Through the kindness of a friend in Philadelphia, I have recently come into possession of an original document, purporting to be an agreement or contract between the building committee of the congregation and the carpenters by whom the old Meeting-House that was burned down in 1780 was built." The agreement which follows bears date "this twenty-fourth day of February, Anno Domini, 1723-4, and in the tenth year of our sovereign Lord King George, &c.," and is signed by John Thompson, Nathaniel Bonnell, Joseph Woodruff, David Morehouse, Nathaniel Bonnell, Jr. "A committee chosen by the Presbyterian Society of Elizabeth Town for taking care of building a Meeting-House for said society." "It will thus be seen," as Dr. Hatfield adds, "that the house was built in the summer of 1724, and was 58 feet in length and 42 feet in width; and that the audience room was 24 feet in height. * * An addition to the length in the rear of 16 feet was made in 1766, so that its final dimensions were 74 by 42 feet."

The lot on which the house was built included the present burying-ground, and extended on the West to the river (so called), and contained about eight acres. When the church property was surveyed in 1766, the Trustees affirmed "that the first purchasers and associates did give the aforesaid tract of land for the use of the Presbyterian Church, the record of which, on or about the year 1719, was either lost or destroyed." This statement was admitted by the Town Committee, and has constituted the only title of record to the present church property for over a century and a half. The meeting-house occupied the site of the present church, but, as it was much smaller, it did not cover

9

much, if any, more than the front half, the other half containing the graves of most of the first settlers. Graves were sometimes dug under the floor of the church, a custom familiar to the early settlers, and made dear by association with the habits of their ancestors in England, so that nearly the whole area of this church in which we are now gathered, is probably occupied with the dust which awaits the archangel's trump, of the first two or three generations of the people of the town. It is probable that for a long time the church and adjoining burial-ground was not enclosed, or if at all, only in a rude way. In 1762, immediately after the settlement of Rev. Mr. Caldwell, it was voted by the Trustees that "the burial-ground be enclosed with a close, cedar-board fence; also agreed that a neat pale-fence be built to enclose a court-yard in the front and south end of the church."

We may gather some idea of the appearance of the interior of the church at the time it was destroyed, from the directions given by the Trustees to the new sexton, William Woodruff, elected March, 1766 : " Once every three months the alleys below the pulpit-stairs and gallery-stairs must be washed out and well sanded. For evening lectures you are to get the candles, such as the Trustees shall direct, and illuminate the church in every part, and at the conclusion of prayer before sermon, you are immediately to go up and snuff the pulpit candles and the rest of the candles in the church. When you judge the sermon to be about half finished, you are once more to snuff the candles in the pulpit, and at the Clerk's desk." (The most serious objection to this rule, would be the suspicion that the sexton might be open to outside influences to snuff the candles prematurely.) "You are to be very careful of the silk hangings and cushions, that they receive no injury by dust spots. You are to see that the pulpit door be always opened ready for the minister's entrance, and the bible opened on the cushion. You are to prevent, as much as in you lies, all undue noises and disorders, and suffer no *white boys* or girls to be standing or sitting on the gallery or pulpit stairs, and if at any time you cannot prevent unruly behavior during divine service, you are immediately to step to one of the Magistrates or Elders present, and inform them of the same. You are weekly to wind up and regulate the church-clock." Such, as nearly as we are able to present it to you, was the venerable church edifice in its external and internal appearance, and in its surroundings. "The church in which Caldwell preached," says Dr. Murray in his notes, "was cheerfully yielded as a hospital for sick and disabled and wounded soldiers, as some of the aged ones yet among us testify ; it was its bell that sounded through the town the notes of alarm on the approach of the foe; its floor was not unfrequently the bed of the weary soldier, and the seats of its pews the table from which he ate his scanty meal."

Sad, sad indeed, to the hearts of parents and children who were wont to gather here to worship the God of their fathers, were the tidings which on the 26th of January, 1780, rapidly spread throughout the scattered congregation, that, of the dear old church, nothing now was left but a heap of ashes. But the faith in God and the love of liberty, which had been taught for generations in that venerable edifice, were lodged *in the hearts* of that congregation beyond the reach of the Tory's torch. And the cowardly act of

11

wanton destruction of the house-of-worship so dear to them, only *fired their hearts* to more absolute sacrifice of whatever should be demanded to make good before the world that Declaration of Independence of British rule to which one of their own members had signed his name, and *nerved their arms* to strike with heavier blow, until by God's blessing, independence achieved, they could again erect over the ashes of their dead, and over the ashes of their humble "meeting-house," a house of worship. None will question that the character of the men who laid the foundations of the Colonies which became the United States of America, had very much to do in determining the views and principles of their descendants who united in the grand struggle of the Revolution. This was emphatically the case in regard to the early settlers of Elizabeth Town, one of the first points occupied in the history of New Jersey. On the 28th day of October, 1664, a tract of land, about 500,000 acres, embracing the whole of what are now the counties of Union, Morris, and part of Essex and Somerset, was purchased of the Indians by John Baker, John Ogden, John Bayley and Luke Watson, who acted for themselves and their associates. This purchase was made by these men, who were residents of Long Island, with reference to a speedy settlement upon the purchase. " It is safe to conclude," says Dr. Hatfield, "that ground was broken for the settlement of the town as early as in November, 1664, and that in the spring of 1665 a considerable number of the associates for whom the land had been purchased, arrived with their wives and children, and took possession of their new homes in Achter Kol," the name given by the Dutch to Newark

Bay, meaning "behind the bay," and also extended to the region West of the North River. The same year, 1664, the Duke of York having by patent from Charles II. the right of sale, conveyed to Lord Berkeley and Sir George Carteret, who were of the Court of Charles, the territory lying to the West of the Hudson and East of the Delaware, known as Nova Cæserea, or New Jersey (after the isle of Jersey, of which Carteret's father was Deputy Governor.) Capt. Philip Carteret, a distant relative of Sir George, was sent out to become Governor of the territory for the Proprietors. He arrived at what is known in history as Elizabeth Town Point in August, 1665, and was well received by Ogden and his associates, from whom he purchased an interest in the land, recognizing the validity of the grant made by Gov. Nicholls, which confirmed to Ogden and his friends the purchase from the Indians. At this time, as is probable, the town received its name Elizabeth Town from 'Elizabeth,' the name of the wife of Sir George Carteret. Philip Carteret, who was henceforth called Gov. Carteret, was a young man of about 26 years of age when he arrived. He married in 1681 the widow of Capt Lawrence of Long Island; she had at that time seven children; two of them died here in 1687, and were buried in the church-yard; their monuments may be seen to-day set in the rear wall of this building, and serve as history written in stone, of exceeding interest. In the plan for the government of New Jersey, conveyances and agreements were laid down "to and with all and every of the adventurers, and all who shall settle and plant there," which instrument accorded "the utmost freedom of conscience, consistent with the preservation of the public peace and order, in matters pertaining to religion, and provided every practicable safeguard for political freedom." It committed the work of legislation and taxation to a Legislature, of which the popular branch were to be chosen directly by the people; and thus early established in this favored Colony the doctrine, for which a century later the combined Colonies so strenuously and successfully contended, that there shall be *no taxation without representation*, that the *people* must have a direct voice in the raising and expending of money for government, a doctrine of which John Bright said the other day in a speech, that in contending against it in the war of the American Revolution, "the folly, the tyranny of George III. and his ministers, and the perverse obstinancy of their majority in Parliament, laid the foundation of the American Republic." A doctrine thus handed down by their forefathers, the men and women who worshiped the God of their fathers in the old church of 1780, true to their sacred trust, maintained with unyielding steadfastness throughout eight years of war, at the sacrifice of husbands and sons, of their Pastor and his wife, of their house of worship, their parsonage, and in instances not a few, of their own homes; and in the end *they prevailed* "because they relied upon the Lord God of their fathers."

The early settlers of this town were almost wholly New Englanders, from Long Island and Connecticut. At a town meeting of the Freeholders and inhabitants of Elizabeth Town, held February 19th, 1665, it was resolved "that the aforesaid town shall consist of four score families for the present." These constituted the original *Associates*: their names

to the number of sixty-five are appended to the oath
of allegiance to King Charles II., taken at the same
town meeting. A biographical sketch of each of these
Associates, founders of the town, is given in Dr. Hatfield's history, the remarkable result of long, patient
and minute investigation, for which very few men
were so extraordinarily qualified as he. "Of these
men" he says, "a large proportion, nearly all, had
brought their wives with them; some of them had
several children also; a small number were considerably in years. The most of them, however, were
young, vigorous, robust men, between the ages of
twenty-five and forty, just the men to lay the foundations of many generations." The town was founded,
not by Carteret, but by Ogden, Watson, Baker and their
personal friends. Among them we find names such as
Ogden, Crane, Mosse (or Morse), Tucker, Price, Bunnell,
Whitehead, Heathfield (or Hatfield), Meacker, Barber,
and others, which have been familiar "as household
words" in this community for two centuries. They
were neighbors and friends who had intermarried, and
when they met here they met as old acquaintances, as
one people. "The planters of this town had, the most
of them, been nurtured under the Commonwealth.
They had learned almost from their earliest days to abjure the divine right of kings, and to regard the House
of Stuart with holy aversion, as invaders of the vested
rights of the people, and as essentially imperious
despots. They had been trained to the largest liberty
in government. They met and deliberated, made and
administered the laws, and took measures for the welfare of the people, with none to molest or 'make them
afraid.' The descendants of such men were the patriots

of the Revolutionary War. Carteret and his company, on the other hand, were Monarchists; diligently and sacredly taught to believe in the divine right of kings; to be jealous for the royal prerogative; to hate and abjure both Cromwell and the Commonwealth; to look with contempt upon the 'round-heads,' and to make sport of Puritan strictness in religion and morals."

Thus was established in the early settlement of the town, what might be called a Court party. Collisions between them and their descendants, with the more democratic sons of New England, were to be expected; and they came in the days that tried men's souls in the struggle for Independence. Bitter, bitter indeed were the oppositions of sentiment, and severe the retaliatory acts which divided in this community for many years, kinsmen and fellow citizens. On the one hand, royalists and refugees escaping to Staten Island, to be under the British flag; and on the other, Caldwell and the devoted patriots who followed his leading; defending as best they could from behind stone and rail fences, or on open field, through summer heats and winter snows, through loss of property and of life, the doctrines and traditions so dear to their ancestors, which were embodied in the Declaration of Independence.

One of the most influential founders of the town, the man who left the strongest imprint of his own sterling character upon the little community, and one whose numerous descendants to this day make mention of with honorable pride, was JOHN OGDEN, one of the four original Patentees. He was born in Stamford, Connecticut, and came to this place from Northampton, Long Island. " He was among the very first, with his five full grown boys, John, Jonathan, David, Joseph and Benjamin, to remove to the new purchase and erect a dwelling. A true patriot, and a genuine Christian, he devoted himself while living to the best interests of the town; and dying, bequeathed to his sons the work of completing what he had so fairly and effectually inaugurated, *the establishment of a rigorous plantation founded on the principles of civil and religious liberty.*"

Having sought to trace up to their fountain head, —viz., the character of the men who laid the foundation stones of this community,—those influences which wrought through successive generations to make the congregation which worshiped on this spot in 1780 almost a unit in supporting the Declaration of Independence, it will be necessary to pass more rapidly over the events which followed, and to confine our attention for a few moments more immediately to the concerns of the church itself. It cannot be determined with exactness who served the people as Pastor, or pulpit supply, for the first few years from the date of the first settlement. Dr. Hatfield says "it is safe to conclude that Mr. Jeremiah Peck came to this town from Newark as early as 1668, on invitation of the people, to serve them in the ministry of the gospel, and that he is to be regarded as the first Pastor of the church in this place." In the autumn of 1678, he accepted a call to Greenwich, Conn. He was succeeded in 1680 by Rev. Seth Fletcher. He came from Southampton, and became Minister of this town in the summer or autumn of 1680. His death occurred in August, 1682. For five years subsequent to his death, the church was without a Pastor. On September 30th, 1687, the Rev. John Harriman was installed Pastor of this church; he died here in August, 1705, and his monument stands in the adjoining church-yard. Soon after his entering on the pastoral work here, he opened an account with every one of the subscribers to his support. These accounts were kept in two books; the second, from 1694 to 1705, is now in possession of the Session. The whole number of actual subscribers was 124. The subscriptions amounted to £83 11s. 0d. A very small part only of the subscriptions were paid in cash, the most of them are credited with produce, meat, grain, and vegetables; many of them with labor by the day on the farm, or in building or repairing his house or barn. The work of a Pastor was evidently not so circumscribed as at the present day. Besides preaching, pastoral visitation, farming, carrying on a flour mill and a cider press, Mr. Harriman had an agency for furnishing glass to his neighbors. He surveyed lands now and then, he attended the Legislature as a Deputy through four years, and like most of his profession in those days, he kept a boarding-school; he dealt also considerably in real-estate. We find the following entry in his account book, suggestive of an institution then almost universally recognized in the Colonies, the wiping out of which has but just cost our country, in blood and treasure, a price immeasurably beyond that of the Independence of the Colonies—and to aid in this glorious result, not a few here carried a musket under the old flag before us—I mean *slavery.* "We bought the negro Toney, August 14th, 1697, of Charles Tooker, Jr., for £18," and again "October 20th, 1701, bought of Mr. James Evert an Indian girl named Hagar, for £19 10s." During the conflict from 1688 to 1702, between the inhabitants of the town and the so called Proprietors, which was at one time so bitter as to be properly called "revolutionary," and was terminated by the arrival of a royal commission in 1703, bringing to a perpetual end the Proprietary Government of East Jersey, Mr. Harriman stood bravely forth as the representative of popular rights, and in his discourses from the pulpit, as well as in his daily intercourse with the people, set the example of resistance to oppression, and maintenance of the just rights of the people, which was followed so zealously by Caldwell in 1776.

During the ministry of Rev. Samuel Melyen, who succeeded Mr. Harriman, the first Episcopal congregation of this town was gathered; the Episcopal portion of the community having been contented for forty years to worship with their Puritan neighbors, beside whom also, when their life-work was done, they were content to lie in the old church-yard, where to-day occasionally are interred, beside the dust of their honored ancestors, the descendants of Episcopal families, resident here before the foundations of St. John's Church were laid.

The ministry of Mr. Melyen was short. The church did not remain long without a Pastor; for on the 29th of September, 1709, Jonathan Dickinson was ordained and installed as pastor of this church.* He was born April 22, 1688, at Hatfield, Mass. His early life was mostly spent in Springfield. Yale College went into operation in 1702; young Dickinson entered the College the same year, and was graduated in 1706. Concerning his theological studies, and his licensure to preach, we have no information. He came here in 1708, being then not quite twenty-one years of age.

* The following sketch of the life and work of Dickinson was not delivered with the discourse, but is inserted here in order to complete the history of the church during the century.

He was ordained, after preaching here for a short time, by a Council of Congregational Ministers from Stamford, Fairfield and Norwalk, Ct. His field of labor extended as far to the West as Westfield. "Neither church nor minister was yet to be found in the regions beyond toward the setting sun. It was the extreme border of civilization. It was a weighty charge to be laid on such youthful shoulders. Quietly and diligently he applied himself to his work, and his profiting presently appeared to all. It was not long before he took rank among the first of his profession."

Previous to Dickinson's settlement as Pastor, this church had been Independent or Congregational, in its form of government; not until forty years after its organization was the first Presbytery, the Presbytery of Philadelphia, constituted. Dickinson, whose sympathies were probably quite decidedly with Presbyterianism, proceeded with a wise caution in the matter of bringing his church into connection with Presbytery, for his people "were thorough Puritans and men of spirit, and slow to part with what they conceived to be their rights." It is probable that he united with the Presbytery of Philadelphia in the Spring of 1717, and that the church soon after joined the same Presbytery. In the following year, September 19, 1718, it is noted in the records of Synod that "Mr. Dickinson delivered one pound twelve shillings from his congregation of Elizabeth Town for the fund 'for pious uses.'" "This," says Dr. Hatfield, "was undoubtedly the first contribution for Presbyterian purposes ever made by this congregation." The church was represented in Synod for the first time in 1721, by one of their elders, Robert Ogden, a grandson of "Old John Ogden." It is worthy of remark in passing, that having been chosen Moderator of Synod for that year, in his opening sermon before Synod the following year he discussed the question of ecclesiastical jurisdiction; a "vexed question" at that time between those who favored on the one hand the more rigid, or on the other the more liberal application of the Presbyterian system. In a paper which was prepared by Dickinson, and unanimously adopted by Synod, "the power of the keys is accorded to the church officers, and to them only; care is taken to distinguish between legislative acts binding on the conscience, and orderly regulations conformed to God's word; and the right of appeal from the lower to the higher Court is admitted." We mention this as showing that the same jealous regard for the rights of the people, ecclesiastical as well as civil, which had characterized this congregation from its infancy, was still maintained by Pastor and people, and continued to exercise a moulding influence which told most effectively upon the attitude of the congregation when the hour arrived in which their descendants were called upon to decide for or against the Declaration of Independence. The influence of Dickinson, and his hold upon the confidence and respect of the church at large, increased every year. His constitutional love of liberty, and unwillingness to impose as binding upon others, creeds or confessions which he himself could freely adopt, led him to oppose with all the weight of his great influence in the Synod of 1729 a proposition to require of every minister and candidate a hearty assent to the Westminster Confessions and Catechisms. But he succeeded, as before, by the exercise of practical wisdom and Christian forbearance in uniting the action of Synod in favor of the measure proposed by him, and known afterward as "the Adopting Act."

In the controversy with the East Jersey Proprietors, he took an active part in aiding his people in defending their claims to their property, and proved himself to be "an invaluable counselor and organizer in defense of popular rights; ever standing with his people in all the straits and trials growing out of the litigations with which they were so sorely disturbed." Amidst his arduous labors as a Pastor, he found time to give some attention to the study of medicine, and "acquired a high reputation as a Physician."

Dickinson sought to oppose, with all his ability, the spirit of scepticism which was prevalent at that time, being made fashionable through the writings of Hobbes and Tindal, and others. He preached a series of discourses upon "The Reasonableness of Christianity" which were published in 1732, and are spoken of as "truly admirable discourses, learned, discriminating and logical; full of pith and power; pointed and impressive." As a controvertist, both in matters of religious doctrine and forms of church-government, Jonathan Dickinson had few equals in the church in his day. His writings were widely circulated, and as widely praised. In 1738 he published "The Reasonableness of Nonconformity to the Church of England, in Point of Worship," and in 1741 "The True Scripture Doctrine concerning some important Points of Christian Faith." This work has repeatedly been reprinted in Great Britain and America. In order to meet the feeling of opposition to "the great awakening," he prepared and published at Boston in 1742 "A Display of God's Special Grace, in a familiar dialogue between a minister and a gentlemen of his congregation, about the Work of God in the Conviction and Conversion of Sinners." "No contemporaneous publication" says President Green, "was probably as much read or had as much influence." In 1745 he wrote "Familiar Letters to a Gentleman, upon a variety of Seasonable and Important Subjects in Religion." This book has remained among the standard works on the evidences of Christianity, and the doctrine of God's sovereign grace in the redemption of man. It has been frequently reprinted at home and abroad, and may be found to-day on the catalogue of the Presbyterian Board of Publication. Many of his discourses upon special occasions, and pamphlets upon interesting topics of the day, were also published at different times.

Notwithstanding the multitude of subjects which claimed his attention as a Pastor and author, he became deeply interested in the condition of the Indians in New Jersey and the adjacent Provinces. After his removal to New Jersey, David Brainerd, the devoted Apostle to the Indians, "found in Mr. Dickinson a faithful counselor and devoted friend, and in his house an ever-welcome home. Here—during his last winter on earth—he remained for nearly six months, in so low a state much of the time that his life was almost despaired of."

It was mainly through the influence of Mr. Dickinson that an effort was made toward establishing a College in New Jersey. It is stated that he had for years taught a classical school himself, or at least had received young men into his family who were studying for the ministry. The project of a College was laid before Synod in 1739, and a committee was appointed, of which Mr. Dickinson was a member, to obtain aid from Great Britain. An application for "a Charter to incorporate sundry persons to form a College" was made and granted under the great seal of the Province of New Jersey, October 29, 1746. Under this Charter Mr. Dickinson was appointed one of the "Trustees of the said College." On April 20, 1747, the following notice appeared in the New York Weekly *Post Boy:* "This is to inform the Publick, That the Trustees of the Colledge of New Jersey, have appointed the Rev. Mr. Jonathan Dickinson, *President* of the said Colledge; which will be opened the fourth week in May next, at Elizabeth Town; at which time and place all Persons suitably qualified, may be admitted to an Academic Education."

At the time specified, the first term of the College of New Jersey was opened at Mr. Dickinson's house, on the south side of the old Rahway Road, directly West of Race Street. Among the first graduates of the Institution—which as Princeton College, stands to-day in the very front rank of American Colleges, an honor to the State, and the object of a just pride and affection on the part of its numerous alumni—were the Rev. Hugh Henry, Richard Stockton of Princeton, and Rev. Daniel Thane, afterward Pastor of the church of Connecticut Farms. These had all been under the instruction of Mr. Dickinson.

The laying of the foundations of this noble Institution seems to have been reserved in the providence of God, for the crowning work of a life of eminent usefulness. On the seventh day of October of the same year, 1747, having finished his work on earth, he entered into rest. For forty years he had served Christ as Pastor of this

24

church. A man endowed of God with great and unusually versatile talent, his life-work bore testimony to the unreservedness of his consecration of all his gifts to the service of Christ through the church he loved. As an expression of the esteem in which he was held by his contemporaries, we feel constrained to make room, just here, for the following notice of his death and burial which appeared in the New York Weekly *Post Boy* of October 12, 1747:

Elizabethtown in New Jersey, Oct. 10.

On Wednesday Morning last, about 4 o'clock, died here of a pleuritic illness, that eminently learned, faithful and pious Minister of the Gospel, and President of the College of New Jersey, the Rev. Mr. Jonathan Dickinson, in the 60th Year of his Age, who had been Pastor of the First Presbyterian Church in this Town for nearly forty Years, and was the Glory and Joy of it. In him conspicuously appeared those natural and acquired moral and spiritual Endowments which constitute a truly excellent and valuable Man, a good Scholar, an eminent Divine, and a serious devout Christian. He was greatly adorned with the Gifts and Graces of his Heavenly Master, in the Light whereof he appeared as a Star of superior Brightness and Influence in the Orb of the Church, which has sustained a great and unspeakable Loss in his Death. He was of uncommon and very extensive Usefulness. He boldly appeared in the Defence of the great and important Truths of our most holy Religion and the Gospel Doctrines of the free and sovereign Grace of God. He was a zealous Promoter of godly Practice and godly Living, and a bright Ornament to his Profession. In Times and Cases of Difficulty he was a ready, wise and able Counsellor. By his Death our infant College is deprived of the Benefit and Advantage of his superior Accomplishments, which afforded a favorable Prospect of its future Flourishing and Prosperity under his Inspection. His remains were decently interred here Yesterday, when the Rev. Mr. Pierson, of Woodbridge, preached his funeral Sermon, and as he lived desired of all so never any Person in these Parts died more lamented. Our fathers where are they and the Prophets, do they live forever?

To the above testimony may be added such words as those of Jonathan Edwards who called him "the late learned and very excellent Mr. Jonathan Dickinson." The Rev. Dr. Bellamy called him "the great Mr. Dickinson." The Rev. Dr. John Erskine, of Edinburgh, said, "The British Isles have produced no such writers on divinity in the eighteenth century as Dickinson and Edwards." "It may be doubted," says Dr. Sprague in his "Annals," "whether with the single exception of the elder Edwards, Calvinism has ever found an abler or more efficient champion in this country than Jonathan Dickinson." "His name," says Dr. Hatfield, "during the nearly forty years of his ministry, gave the town itself a prominence both in the province and in the country."

The Rev. Elihu Spencer began to supply the pulpit in the spring of 1749. He remained Pastor of this church about seven years. Soon after his departure, Rev. Abraham Kettletas supplied the pulpit. His ministry continued nearly three and a half years. The accounts of the treasurer of the congregation, Samuel Woodruff, show that the salary of Mr. Kettletas was paid by regular weekly contributions on the Sabbath. They also show that in the spring of 1759, the belfry of the church was provided with a town-clock, probably for the first time; at whose expense it was provided is left to conjecture. It had but one face, fortunately for the community, and therefore could not accomplish the marvelous but disappointing feat, of presenting at a given hour of the day four different indexes of time upon four different faces, as has been frequently done by the ingenious contrivance which at present occupies its place. The same old account book tells other tales. In several places is found a charge as follows: "To one quart of rum 1s. 4d., supplied to the men repairing the old church," and in "June 24th, 1758, two quarts of rum at 2s. 8d., for ye people to pry up the sleepers." We presume that—to borrow Dr. Hatfield's expression elsewhere—it might be "left to conjecture" whether the reference in this charge is to "sleepers" in the pews who might require a little prying up, or, as is more probable, to give Dr. Hatfield's own construction, to the fact "that the floor of the old edifice had begun very seriously to feel the effects of age." Mr. Kettletas resigned his pastoral charge in July, 1760, and was succeeded, after a vacancy in the pulpit of a year and a half, by the Rev. James Caldwell. Mr. Caldwell was a Virginian, born in Charlotte County, in what was then a wilderness, in April, 1734. The place was generally known as the Caldwell settlement. It may be interesting to add that a niece of his was the mother of the Hon. John Caldwell Calhoun of South Carolina, the well-known Senator and prominent statesman of the South. Mr. Caldwell graduated at the College of New Jersey, was licensed to preach the gospel by the Presbytery of New Brunswick in 1760, and accepted a call from this church in November, 1761. He was at that time in the twenty-seventh year of his age, "a young man of prepossessing appearance, and of more than ordinary promise as a preacher of the gospel." Mr. Caldwell was married just one year after his entering upon his pastoral charge, to Hannah, daughter of John Ogden of Newark. Her father was the great-grandson of the John Ogden of whom we have spoken as one of the first settlers of the town. During the first year of his settlement the "Apostolic Whitfield" preached here twice on the Sabbath of November 27th, 1763, as he had done before in the days of Dickinson, and as had also David Brainerd often done. We may remark in passing, that we can trace up to about this date the origin of two customs in our churches, viz., the raising of the current expenses of the church by pew-rents, and singing by choirs. Up to this time current expenses had been met by Sabbath collections, and all singing in the churches was congregational, led by a Precentor. In May, 1767, it was resolved "to offer the pews in the enlarged building at public vendue, agreeable to certain fixed rates, the rents to be paid quarterly." "There were few country churches with a choir before 1765 or 1770, and they certainly did not become common until the time of the American Revolution." It may be worthy of remark as illustrating the cyclical tendency of all things in the affairs of men, as in the world of nature, that during the century embraced within the dates of 1770 and 1870, all the known methods of conducting and aiding the musical part of church service, including large voluntary choirs, a selected quartette choir with liberal salary, organ, bass-viols (the introduction of which so aroused at the time the righteous indignation of one of the oldest Elders of the church), and clarionets, with other brass instruments, have been tried by this church; returning at last to the "old way of the fathers," congregational singing with a Precentor. If, however, the theory of cyclical movement be correct, we may "expect about this time" as the Farmers' Almanac has it, "a change of some kind."

We must hasten to enter upon the stormy period of the War of the Revolution, in which Pastor and people in this old historic church were to take so signal a part. The parish of Mr. Caldwell included the whole of Elizabeth Town, and the town included nearly the whole of the present Union County; the towns of Union, Springfield, New Providence, Westfield, Plainfield, Rahway, Linden, and Clark, having since been organized out of the ancient territorial domain of Elizabethtown. The old book to which I have referred, shows that in 1776, there were three hundred and forty-five pew-renters and subscribers in the congregation. The Ruling Elders at that time were Cornelius Heatfield, John Potter, Samuel Williams and Benjamin Winans; Isaac Woodruff, Jonathan Williams, Caleb Halstead, David Ogden, Isaac Arnett, Jonathan Price, Trustees. In the congregation, at the opening of the Revolution, were such men as William Livingston, the noble Governor of the State, who, through a storm of obloquy from some of his former friends, and of bitter and unrelenting hatred and plottings against his life on the part of the Tories and the British, remained steadfast in his devotion to the cause of freedom, to the final victory. Elias Boudinot, who served on the Staff of Gen. Livingston; was appointed by Congress Commissary-General of prisoners; was Member of Congress in 1778, 1781 and 1782; chosen

President of Congress Nov. 2, 1782, and when the treaty of peace with Great Britain was ratified, April 15th, 1783, he had the honor of affixing to it his signature. He received from Yale College in 1790 the degree of Doctor of Laws; was a Trustee of the College of New Jersey for twenty-three years, and in 1816 the first President of the American Bible Society. In forwarding from Philadelphia, while Superintendent of the Mint, as a gift to the Trustees of the First Presbyterian Church, a pair of elegant and costly cut-glass chandeliers, he said, in his letter bearing date Feb. 26th, 1800, of the church: "The many happy hours I have spent there, make the remembrance of having been one of their Society, among the substantial pleasures of my life." In the congregation at this time also, was Abraham Clark, one of the Signers of the Declaration of Independence; he had long been a member of the Church, and was one of its Trustees from 1786 to 1790. He was chosen seven times as a delegate from New Jersey to the Continental Congress. Here, also, were the Hon. Robert Ogden (Speaker of the Assembly at an earlier day), with his three sons, Robert, Matthias and Aaron, the last two distinguished officers in the U. S. Army; the Hon. Stephen Crane, Speaker of the Assembly; Elias Dayton, and his son Jonathan, both of them subsequently general officers of the Army, and the latter Speaker of Congress; William Peartree Smith, one of the most distinguished civilians of the day; Oliver Spencer and Francis Barber, both of them Colonels of the Jersey Brigade, from whom Gen. Maxwell, Commandant of the Brigade, received on all occasions, and some of them of a trying nature, most zealous and efficient co-operation; and other such devoted patriots, not a few.

"From this one congregation went forth *over forty commissioned officers* of the Continental Army, not to speak of non-commissioned officers and privates, to fight the battles of Independence." The names of thirty-nine of them are given in a foot-note in Dr. Hatfield's History. An honor roll, of which the old First Church, with all her children, has a right to be proud to-day! These were the men who, with their neighbors and friends, their wives, children and grandchildren were worshiping the God of their fathers in the venerable shingle-covered church, when, upon their ears fell the announcement, startling as the alarm-bell at night, that the British Parliament had passed, in March 1764, a resolution declaring the intention of Government to raise a revenue in America by a duty on stamped paper. Of these men, Dr. Hatfield says: "The love of civil and religious liberty and the hatred of despotism, they had inherited as almost their only heritage." But there was a special reason why this odious Stamp-Act aroused in this community a peculiar determination to resist its enforcement to the bitter end; for in it was violated a fundamental principle of the Constitution, under which they and their fathers had been born and nurtured. It was provided by the concessions of Berkley and Carteret, in respect to the Governor and Council, that "they are not to impose, nor suffer to be imposed, any tax, custom, subsidy, tallage, assessment, or any other duty whatsoever, upon any colour or pretense, upon the said province and inhabitants thereof, other than what shall be imposed by the authority and consent of the General Assembly." When, therefore, the ringing voice of James Otis, of Massachusetts Colony, was heard proclaiming throughout the Colonies, the doctrine that "Civil government is of God, and the original possessors of power are the whole people, and that under the British Constitution the Colonists enjoyed the right in their local legislatures of *governing themselves*" a doctrine which was soon condensed into the popular apothegm, "no representation, no tax,"—it is no strange thing (when parties arose, as at once they did, those on the one side, called Whigs, Patriots, Sons of Liberty; those on the other, Loyalists, Tories and Friends of Government,) that the "Sons of Liberty" were found here, both numerous and ready for prompt action. The Act was to take effect November 1st, 1765, but not a stamp was to be found in the town, nor was it safe either to offer for sale, or to use one, as the following extract from a New York paper of February 27th, 1766, would plainly indicate: "A large gallows was erected in Elizabethtown last week, with a rope ready fixed thereto, and the inhabitants there vow and declare that the first person that either takes out or distributes a stamped paper, shall be hung thereon without judge or jury."

When the vindictive Act of the British Parliament, closing the port at Boston, in retaliation for the "Boston Tea Party" was passed, the patriotic spirit of the Colonists broke forth in a flame of angry resentment. Nowhere was the spirit of resistance to tyranny more manifest than in this town, which became from that time the headquarters of the patriot movement in New Jersey. Then was heard from Sabbath to Sabbath in the old Church, from the Pastor, the earnest prayer to Almighty God, the Ruler of Nations, and the Defender of the right, that he would give to the congregation assembled here, unity in counsel, and courage of heart to do and to dare in defense of the sacred principles of liberty bequeathed to them in trust by their ancestors. And as the cloud appeared which was soon to roll up, black with the coming storm of war, and charged with the lightnings of man's wrath, which would, before it was passed, sweep away Pastor, and Church and Parsonage, in a common destruction, Caldwell poured out from his pulpit in eloquent utterances, words of faith in God, and uncompromising devotion to the cause so dear to his own heart. Nor did his words fall on ears unwilling to hear, or hearts unsympathetic with his fervent appeals. On the contrary, that people, well trained in the doctrines and promises of God's word, and believing in the "God of their fathers," came forward, as it were with one hand and one purpose; and at the very opening of the conflict, with the calm determination of men who had counted the cost, consecrated their all a *free-will* offering upon the altar of devotion to principle; and then taking down from the wall the old flint-lock musket, and looking it over carefully, patiently awaited the events of the future. Nor did they have to wait long. Blood flowed at Lexington, Mass., on Wednesday, the 19th of April, 1775. That "blood cried from the ground," and its voice was heard in every hamlet and every home of the United Colonies. The tidings reached New Jersey on the following day; the whole community was aroused, the excitement was intense. Patient endurance of wrong at the hands of a Government which the Colonists had dearly loved, and from which they had a right to expect fostering care, had now ceased to be a virtue. The sacred cause of

33

American Independence had received its first baptism of blood. "Oh, what a glorious morning is this," exclaimed Samuel Adams, of Massachusetts, when he heard the guns at Lexington. "It was not safe," says Dr. Hatfield, in that hour when the echo passed over New Jersey, "to breathe a word in Elizabethtown against the patriot cause." When the tidings of the Declaration of Independence reached this town "the great majority of the people hailed it with joy, and accepted the arbitrament of the sword with calm determination; some, however, took the first opportunity to connect themselves, openly and violently, with the cause of royalty." By the occupation in the Summer of 1776, of Staten Island, by the British under Gen. Howe, this town was brought into the very fore-front of the field of conflict, and so continued throughout the war. As an illustration of the spirit which inspired parents and children alike, in that hour of anxiety, and uncertainty concerning the future to which this Declaration of Independence would inevitably commit the people, I cannot refrain from quoting an anecdote found in a Philadelphia paper of August 10th, 1776: "On the late alarm at Elizabethtown July 3d, when an immediate attack of the British regulars was expected, and every man capable of bearing arms was summoned to defend it, there were three or four young men, brothers, going out from one house, when an elderly lady, mother or grandmother to the young men, with a resolute calmness, encouraged and assisted them to arm. When they were just setting out, she addressed them thus: 'My children, I have a few words to say to you. You are going out in a just cause, to fight for the rights and liberties of your country; you have my blessing and prayers, that God will protect and assist you; but if you fall, His will be done. Let me beg of you, my children, that if you fall, it may be *like men*, and that if you are found on the battle field, it may be with your wounds in your breast, and not in your back.'" Such was the spirit of the Christian mothers, who sat in God's house on this hallowed ground, in the days of Caldwell and the Revolution. God grant that in this noble union of piety and ardent patriotism, the children who shall from generation to generation occupy these seats, may prove themselves worthy of such mothers.

The Fourth of July, 1776, was celebrated in this town in the following manner, as given in a newspaper of the day, "One of the enemy's armed-sloops of fourteen guns, having this evening run up near Elizabethtown Point, was attacked from the shore, with two twelve-pounders, a great number of her men killed, she set on fire, and entirely destroyed." "As this occurred within two or three hours of the adoption of the Declaration of Independence, it was probably the first military exploit of the new-born nation, and an auspicious omen of its career." In April, 1776, Col. Dayton's regiment, that had been quartered in town, received orders to march for the relief of the army besieging Quebec. As most of the officers, and many of the privates, were members of Mr. Caldwell's congregation, a strong desire was expressed that he should serve as Chaplain. Lieut. Elmer, in his Diary April 28th, says: "Members of the Presbyterian meeting, met about Mr. Caldwell's going to Quebec with us, which was agreed on after some debate." "Parson Caldwell," or the "Fighting Chaplain," as he was called by the British, who had reason both to fear and hate him for his powerful influence in aiding the patriot cause, was from that time forward to the close of his life, occupied more or less continually, in the service of his country. "He was at once the ardent patriot, and the faithful Christian Pastor. The Sabbath found him, whether at home or in the camp, ready to proclaim the Gospel, with its messages of mercy and comfort, to his fellow men; while he was ever watchful at other times to use every opportunity to promote the spiritual welfare of citizens and soldiers. He was held, therefore, in the highest esteem by officers and men, confided in by all, and regarded with enthusiastic love by the rank and file." No one, consequently, save his parishioner, Gov. Livingston, was more feared and hated by the Tories and the British. Gladly would they have kidnapped him if they could. Doubtless it was owing to a full appreciation of this fact, that he was wont, as Dr. McDowell relates, when returning from active service to pass a Sunday with such of his flock as could be gathered in the old Red Store House, to make ready for opening the service by laying his cavalry pistols upon the pulpit cushion, ready for immediate use if required, while sentinels were stationed at the doors to give warning. As the result of the disastrous campaign on Long Island, New York City was abandoned by the American army on September 15th, 1776, and occupied by the British. Then began the retreat of Washington's army into New Jersey. A dark, sad day, was that 28th of November 1776, when Washington, with the wreck of his army, not more than 3,500 in number, entered this town, then almost deserted, and was followed, as the rear guard of the American army left, by the advance guard of Lord Cornwallis. On the 6th of December, Washington writes to Congress, "By a letter of the 14th ultimo from a Mr. Caldwell, a clergyman and a staunch friend to the cause, from Elizabethtown, I am informed that Lord Howe was expected in that town to publish pardon and peace. * * * In the language of this good man, 'The Lord deliver us from his mercy.'"

The dawn of a brighter day for the patriot cause was at hand. On the 26th of December, 1776, Washington captured a force of nearly a thousand Hessians at Trenton; and on the morning of July 3d, 1777, surprised and captured Princeton. Gen. Maxwell followed up these victories by coming down from the Short Hills, with his Jersey Brigade, and driving the British out of Newark and Elizabethtown. When Caldwell and his people returned to their homes in January, 1777, after an exile of six weeks, "they found everything in ruins; their houses plundered, their fences broken down and consumed, their gardens laid waste, their fields an open common, and their records, both public and private, destroyed." Gen. Maxwell, in accordance with Gen. Washington's proclamation, required all who would not take the oath of allegiance, to take themselves and their families off immediately to the enemy. It was a hard case, as the line ran, in some instances, between parents and their children, as well as between brothers and sisters.

During the year 1778, which was one of unusual quiet for the people of this town, an illicit traffic was carried on between the refugees on Staten Island and in New York, and their old neighbors, who had managed to remain in the town. In reply to directions from Washington that this thing *must be stopped*, Gov. Livingston wrote, "Of all those who have applied to me for recommendations to the commanding officer at Elizabethtown to go to New York, not above one in twenty appeared entitled to that indulgence, and many of them were as venomous Tories as any in this country. It is either from a vain curiosity (extremely predominant in women) cloaked with the pretense of securing their debts or effects, in which they seldom if ever succeed, or for the sake of buying tea and trinkets, (for which they would as soon forfeit a second Paradise, as Eve did the first for the forbidden fruit) that they are perpetually prompted to these idle rambles. The men are still more seriously mischievous, and go with commercial motives." It is but simple justice to narrate an incident or two on the other side, as showing in the patriot women of the Revolution something more than "a vain curiosity:" and our first illustration shall be taken from the family of Gov. Livingston himself, whose eldest daughter, when on the night of February 24th, 1779, the British endeavored to take by surprise and capture her father (who fortunately had left home only a few hours before), and breaking into the house at midnight demanded from her his papers, had sufficient presence of mind to lead them into the library and show them a drawer of *intercepted letters from London*, taken in a British vessel, part of which they pocketed, and then carried off the remainder, with the drawer itself; thus adroitly saving others of great value, such as the raiders were in search of. Another proof that *courage* and *wise economy* were combined in the women of those days, is found in the fact that while the Academy, then used as a store-house,

and standing on the spot now occupied by our Lecture-
room, was burning, having been fired the same night
with the just mentioned attempt to capture Gov. Livingston, a Mrs. Egbert, with a few of her female neighbors, rescued from the burning building twenty-six
barrels of flour. With a brief reference to the important events which occurred in the month of June, 1780,
we shall bring to a close this narrative of facts and incidents illustrative of the days of Caldwell and the
Revolution. On the 6th of June, 1780, Gen. Knyphausen, Commander-in-Chief of the British forces in and
around New York, undertook the execution of a carefully prepared plan for capturing or driving out of New
Jersey the patriot army. His confident expectation
was that he would capture Maxwell's Brigade, stationed
at the Short Hills just back of Springfield, and then
proceed against Washington, still in camp at Morristown.
The British troops, about five thousand strong, crossed
the Sound and landed at Elizabeth Town Point, and
passing up Water Street, entered the town just at sun-
rise. The spectacle must have been an imposing one
to the inhabitants of the town, unaccustomed as they
were to "the pomp and circumstance of war." Gen.
Stirling, being the youngest general, led the advance;
Gen. Knyphausen followed at the head of the division.
"An eye witness of the passage of the troops through
the village describes it as one of the most beautiful
sights he ever beheld. In the van marched a squadron
of dragoons of Simcoe's regiment, known as the
Queen's Rangers, with drawn swords and glittering hel-
mets, mounted on very large and handsome horses;
then followed the infantry, composed of Hessians and
English troops, the whole body amounting to nearly

six thousand men, and every man, horseman and foot, clad in new uniforms, complete in panoply, and gorgeous with burnished brass and polished steel." But " let not him that girdeth on his harness boast himself as he that putteth it off." Quickly tidings were sent of the approach of the enemy. The first reception they had was from twelve men who had been stationed at the Crosss Roads to give warning of the approach of the enemy; as they drew near, these men fired upon the advancing officers, and Gen. Stirling fell from his horse severely wounded, they then beat a hasty retreat; an eighteen-pounder signal-gun on Prospect Hill, back of Springfield, was fired; the tar-barrel on the signal-pole was lighted; and as the note of warning reached their ears, the militia, composed of the old farmers and their stalwart sons, instantly dropped the scythe in the field, and seizing the musket from its rack on the wall, began to gather together. There were no feathers in their hats, nor gilt buttons on their home-spun coats, nor flashing bayonets on their old fowling pieces; but there was, in their hearts, the resolute purpose to defend their homes and their liberty at the price of their lives; and by the help of God, they meant to drive these foreign mercenaries, Hessians and men of Waldeck and Anspach, hired by George III. to butcher his own subjects, from Jersey soil as soon as they had set foot upon it. *And they did it* And if occasion should ever require they can do it again. So severe was the annoyance caused by the flank attacks of the unskilled militia, and so determined the resistance made by the small force of regulars under Maxwell, that the enemy were brought to a halt, and the British Commander hearing of the advance of the whole of Washington's force to the Short Hills, a retreat was decided upon and begun at night fall.

In this retreat an act of fiendish barbarity was performed, which brought sore affliction upon Mr. Caldwell and his flock, and intensified to the utmost bitterness the feeling of animosity toward the British soldiers on the part of the inhabitants, many of whom were engaged in the battle. I refer to the cruel and deliberate murder of Mrs. Caldwell, the wife of the Pastor, who was at that time occupying the parsonage at Connecticut Farms with her family of nine children, having been removed thither by Mr. Caldwell for safety. She was sitting in a back room with her children about her, when a British soldier approached the house, and thrusting his musket through the window, shot her dead upon the spot. The few dwellings in this hamlet were plundered of everything portable, and then, together with the Presbyterian Church, were burned to the ground. The expedition proved a miserable failure. The large force of finely mounted and splendidly armed soldiers that in the morning had marched up Water Street in such magnificent and impressive array, had been met, checked, and finally turned back, by a comparative handful of undisciplined, but brave, resolute, determined men ; and that same night, through mud and marsh and in a violent storm of rain, the British forces, chagrined and disgusted to the last degree, regained the point at which they had landed in the morning. ∨ The same experiment was renewed on the 23d of the same month. A force of about five thousand men under Gen. Clinton, crossed over from Staten Island, and passing through the scene of the recent defeat of Knyphausen's forces, they reached

Springfield, where, through the same means of giving warning so successfully used before, they found ready and waiting to give them a like cordial reception, about a thousand men, Continentals and militia combined. A severe engagement followed, in the midst of which, as it is related, Caldwell, finding that the militia were out of wadding for their muskets, galloped to the Presbyterian Church, which was near, and returning with an armful of hymn-books, threw them upon the ground, exclaiming, "Now put Watts into them, boys!" Now, as before, hearing of the approach of Washington, the British set fire to the dwellings and to the church-edifice, and hastily retreated, galled upon flank and rear by the enraged and pursuing militia, who followed them nearly to their fortifications at the Point. The whole of these exploits, from the 7th to the 23d, occurred within the territorial limits of the Old Borough, and among those who contributed, on both occasions, most zealous and effective service, might have been found the patriotic Pastor of the old First Church, and a large proportion of the male members of his congregation. Gen. Washington was delighted with their services, and thus wrote: "The militia deserve everything that can be said; on both occasions they flew to arms universally, and acted with a spirit equal to anything I have seen in the course of the war."

From this time forth the people were mostly permitted to remain at home in the cultivation of their fields, and in the pursuits of trade. Cornwallis surrendered to Washington at Yorktown, October 23d, 1781, and the war of the Revolution was practically at an end. A treaty of peace, based on a full acknowledgment of the Independence of the United States, was signed on the 30th of November, 1782, at Paris, by representatives of Great Britain and the United States. The joy which filled all hearts throughout the United Colonies at the surrender of Cornwallis, was nowhere more sincere or more abounding than in this old Borough, which had been called to make so many and so severe sacrifices for the common cause. But that joy was destined soon to be overshadowed by another dark cloud of affliction. One month after that event which crowned with acknowledged success their long struggle for liberty, Rev. Mr. Caldwell, who had become more and more endeared to the whole community, and was well known and beloved throughout the Province of New Jersey, was on the 24th of November, 1781, cruelly murdered while attending upon a lady who had come over from New York for a visit to her friends in Elizabeth Town, and had landed at the Point. He was shot, without cause or provocation, by a man named Morgan, who had been enlisted as a twelve-months man in the Continental service, and was then acting as a sentinel at the landing at Elizabeth Town Point. In the absence of any ascertained motive for so base a deed, it was quite generally believed that the man had been bribed by British gold. He was tried by court-martial and executed upon the gallows; but he never made any confession of his object, or of what influenced him to the deed. During the funeral services of Mr. Caldwell the whole town suspended business, and expressed in unmistakable manner the deep sorrow that filled all hearts. Surely among the many trying scenes through which the people of this congregation had been called to pass during the War of the Revolution, none could have been more touching and saddening than that which

43

occurred at the funeral, when "after all had taken their last look and before the coffin was closed, Elias Boudinot came forward, leading nine orphan children, and placing them around the bier of their parent, made an address of surpassing pathos to the multitude in their behalf. It was an hour of deep and powerful emotion, and the procession slowly moved to the grave, weeping as they went." Thus had this people been called "to sow in tears," from the day that they rose up as one man, with their beloved Pastor at their head, in response to the call from Lexington, down to the day when just as victory had crowned their sacrifices, they laid their Pastor, cut off in the vigor of full manhood, to rest in the old church-yard.

But these tears were a precursor of a "reaping in joy," not only from the privilege now restored of returning in peace to their homes, and once more setting about rebuilding their house of worship, which they soon did, but from a most precious baptism of the power of the Holy Spirit from on high; as if the "God of their fathers," upon whom they had relied in all their trials, would own with the highest tokens of divine favor the faith in God which had sustained them. It is related that from the time of commencing the work of erecting the church in which we are now assembled, down to its dedication, in an unfinished state, that is from July, 1784, to January, 1786, the congregation was visited with a special outpouring of the Spirit of God. And from that day on to this hour, God, the God of the covenant, the "God of their fathers," has gone before this people, leading them on from generation to generation in the way of loving-kindness and tender mercy; granting to them the inestimable blessing of

44

dwelling together in "the unity of the Spirit and in the bond of peace;" renewing, from time to time, those seasons of spiritual harvesting after years of patient sowing of the seed of divine truth; and permitting us in this day and generation to be so richly the recipients of blessings, temporal and spiritual, vouchsafed to us in answer to the prayers, bequeathed as a precious legacy, of God-fearing, Christ-loving men and women, who through two centuries have worshiped God on this sacred spot, and having served their day and generation have "fallen on sleep."

And now the task assigned me by the Session of this church, and cheerfully accepted, so far as I might be able to meet it, of preparing a discourse which should give in general outline the history of this church from the time of its planting down to the destruction of the church-edifice in 1780, including such events as were of leading interest to this town during the period of the War of the Revolution, is completed. Who can begin to estimate the influence for good upon this community, and upon the surrounding country, of this church, which has just entered upon the third century of its history! From time to time the Mother Church has sent off Colonies to lay the foundations of other Presbyterian churches in this town and vicinity. To-day as they are represented here by their Pastors and members, we declare to them our unfeigned joy over their prosperity, and assure them of our earnest prayers to our Heavenly Father that "grace, mercy, and peace, from God our Father and the Lord Jesus Christ" may abide with them, one and all, even unto the end.

You cannot wonder that the very walls of this venerable Church are dear to her children, not alone to

those now worshiping here, but to those who are removed far away to other parts of the land; and that
every foot of the old grave-yard adjoining, where lies
the dust of the buried generations of their forefathers,
is to them sacred soil. God grant that the generation
now worshiping here, yea, and all that may follow,
may be as sound in doctrine, as fervent in piety, as
loyal to their God, and as true to their country in the
hour of her peril, as were they who here worshiped
God one hundred years ago, from whose lips may have
gone forth the very words of the prophet, "Our holy
and our beautiful house where our fathers praised thee
is burned up with fire, and all our pleasant things are
laid waste;" but who, nevertheless, "strong in the
Lord and in the power of his might" did maintain their
struggle in the sacred cause of a nation's freedom,
through all losses and trials, and in the end "prevailed,
because they relied upon the Lord God of their fathers."

www.ingramcontent.com/pod-product-compliance
Lightning Source LLC
Chambersburg PA
CBHW021430090426
42739CB00009B/1426